W9-DDP-741

DODD, MEAD WONDERLAND BOOKS

THE EVERGLADES: FLORIDA WONDERLAND
GREECE: WONDERLAND OF THE PAST AND PRESENT
HAWAII: PACIFIC WONDERLAND

In the modern city of Athens are these remains of the Temple of the Olympian Zeus, which was completed by the Roman Emperor Hadrian in A.D. 131. Hadrian loved Greece. Near the bottom of the picture is Hadrian's Arch, where important visitors to Athens are officially welcomed.

GREECE

Wonderland of the Past and Present

By Dorothy M. Johnson

ILLUSTRATED WITH PHOTOGRAPHS AND A MAP

Numberless are the world's wonders, but none more wonderful than man.

—SOPHOCLES, 496?-406 B.C.

DODD, MEAD & COMPANY, NEW YORK

Opposite: *The Parthenon, originally a pagan temple, became a Christian church, then a Mohammedan mosque. It was damaged by shellfire in 1687 and again in 1826, during the revolution.*

THIS BOOK IS DEDICATED
TO THE BROWN BROTHERS,
MICHAEL AND KELLY

ACKNOWLEDGMENTS

My thanks to Miss Doreen Magazian, Athens, who answered questions about things that were all Greek to me; Dr. Panos Margaropolous, of the Ministry of Agriculture, for information and courtesy; Dr. George Tsoumis, Pennsylvania State University, for his highly informative manuscript, "Forestry in Greece"; Nick S. Stournaras and his staff for magnificent patience; the Royal Greek Information Service, New York; Trans World Airlines, New York; and various members of the faculty of Montana State University, whose learning is prodigious. I am especially appreciative to Trans World Airlines for the use of the beautiful photograph which appears on the jacket of this book.

CREDITS FOR PHOTOGRAPHS

G. Joakimides, Thera, Santorin, 14; Nick Mavroyenis, Athens, 46, 47; Nick S. Stournaras, Athens, 2, 6, 9, 12, 15, 16, 21, 24, 29, 30, 31, 33, 34, 37, 38, 39, 41, 42, 45, 46, 48, 49, 51, 52, 55, 57, 59, 62; Spyros Meletzis, Athens, 28; Trans World Airlines Photo, 8, 13, 32, 61.

Library of Congress Catalog Card Number: 64-11673
Printed in the United States of America

Contents

An outdoor theater and some pillars of the temple of Apollo at Delphi.

I

The Shape of Greece

One of the most famous rocks in the world is the Acropolis in Athens, capital of Greece. The Acropolis is a plateau 500 feet high, 870 feet long, and 435 feet wide, rising above the modern city.

The first settlers there, nobody knows how long ago, lived on the Acropolis (the name means "high city"), where they could be safe from their enemies. As their village grew, they built homes on the plain below, while on top of the rock they built wonderful marble temples to the gods they worshiped. Still beautiful, even though in ruins now, these temples attract thousands of visitors from all over the world every year, particularly the breath-taking Parthenon which crowns them all.

Athens' seaport is Piraeus, six miles away, a busy city built around a great harbor. Two million people live in Athens and Piraeus. This is one-fourth of the entire population of Greece. The whole country, which includes more than two thousand islands, is about the size of Florida. The Greeks speak of the mainland as Dry Greece and the islands as Wet Greece.

The country is located at the southern tip of the Balkan Peninsula and it is surrounded by seas, except at the north. There, its neighbors are Albania, Yugoslavia, and Bulgaria—all Communist countries now—and a little tip of Turkey, which extends around to the eastern side of the Aegean Sea. Greece and Turkey are free, independent, self-governing nations.

Mainland Greece is broken up by ranges of high mountains, some of them famous in legend and literature. The ancient people said their gods lived on Mount Olympus, in golden palaces built by the smith god, Haephestus. Olympus is a real mountain, 9,570 feet high,

Most famous of the marble temples on the Acropolis in Athens is the Parthenon, honoring Athena, goddess of wisdom. The city was named for her.

in Thessaly. (But Olympia, where the Olympic Games began, is in southern Greece, a long way from the mountain.)

Mount Parnassus, in central Greece, is associated with inspiration for artists, musicians, and writers, because there, legend tells us, the Muses used to live, with the god Apollo as their leader. At Delphi, on Parnassus, you can see the remains of a temple to Apollo that, for a thousand years, attracted visitors who wanted advice. In a hideaway under the temple, a priestess who was called the Oracle used to chew laurel leaves and breathe vapor from a fissure in the rock until she became dizzy. Then, crying and shouting, she answered questions, and the priests told inquirers what she had said and what it meant. They believed that Apollo spoke through her.

More than once, Apollo's temple on Mount Parnassus was destroyed by earthquakes. For hundreds of years, not even any ruins were visible. A village was built there. In the 1890's, the Greek government persuaded the people who lived in it to move a short distance along the mountainside, to a new, pretty village. Archaeologists dug and found the ruins of the temple, an ancient outdoor theater, and a stadium where athletic contests had been held long ago.

Most of the ancient temples throughout Greece were built of marble, which is plentiful in that country. The fine white marble of Mount Pentelikon, eleven miles from Athens, is snowy when it is first cut but changes in time to tawny gold.

Mount Hymettus, also near Athens, is famous for its marble but is even better known for the flavor of the honey made by bees that pasture on the wild flowers that flourish there.

The coast line of Greece is ragged, with many bays and harbors. Before railroads and automobiles were invented, the Greeks found it easier to travel and move freight in ships than by land. The sea is still important for transportation. Almost nobody in Greece lives more than seventy miles from it, and one-sixth of the country consists of islands.

To the west, toward Italy, in the Ionian Sea, is the rocky island of Ithaca, once ruled by a legendary king named Odysseus, or Ulysses. He fought in the Greeks' war against Troy, according to the hero tales, and spent ten years trying to get back home. The story of his adventures is called *The Odyssey*. It is still being enjoyed by many fascinated readers.

At the southern tip of mainland Greece is the island of Cythera. According to myth, Aphrodite, the laughing goddess of love, stepped ashore on this island after she was born of the sea foam. Her Roman name, Venus, is more familiar to us because of a famous marble statue that has lost its arms—the Venus de Milo, in the Louvre in Paris. "Milo" is another name for the island of Melos, in the Aegean Sea, where the statue was found in 1820. The sculptor—nobody knows who he was—lived sometime between 200 and 100 B.C. From

Piraeus is the busy seaport of Athens, capital of Greece.

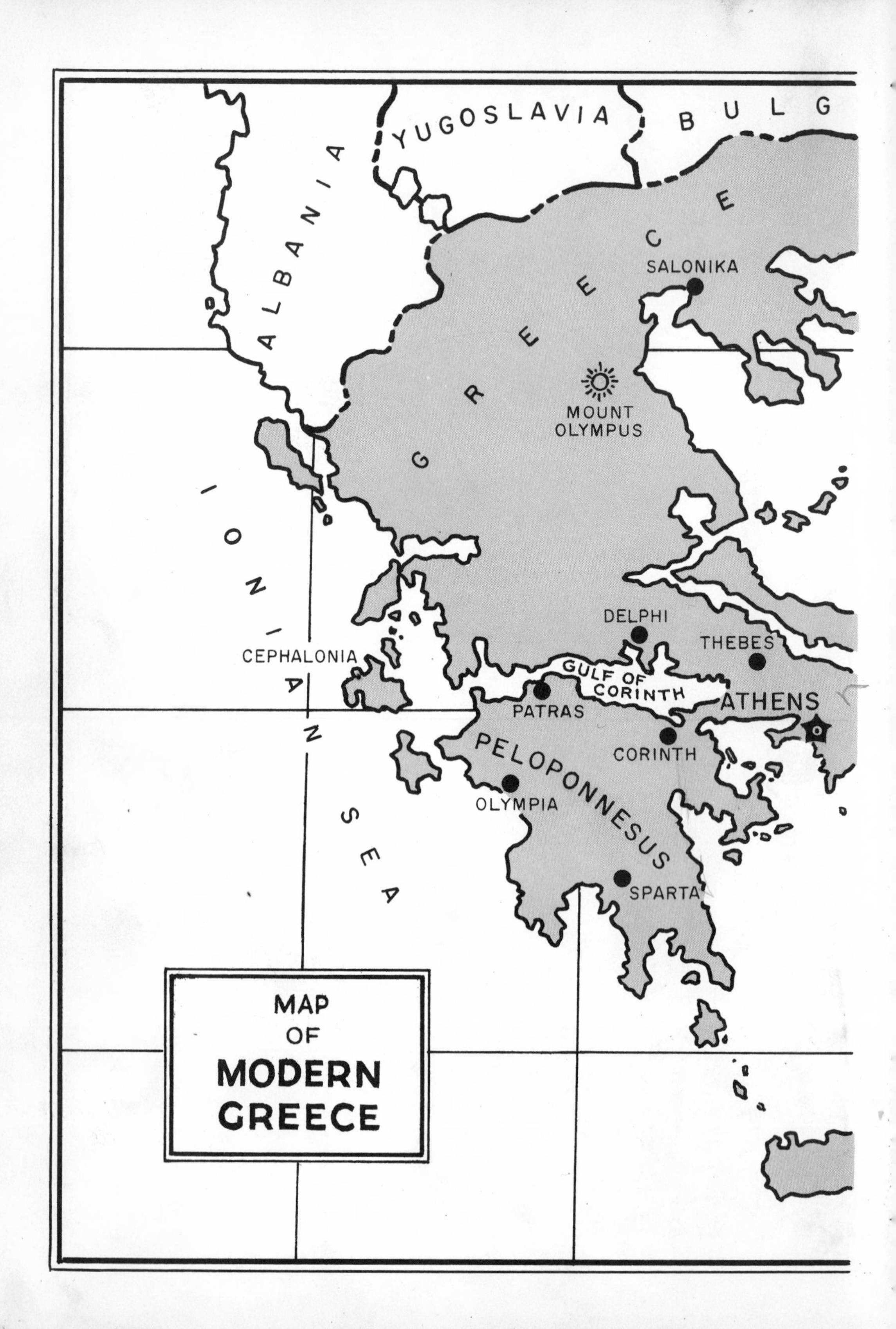
YUGOSLAVIA
BULG
ALBANIA
GREECE
SALONIKA
MOUNT OLYMPUS
IONIAN SEA
DELPHI
THEBES
CEPHALONIA
GULF OF CORINTH
ATHENS
PATRAS
CORINTH
PELOPONNESUS
OLYMPIA
SPARTA
MAP OF MODERN GREECE

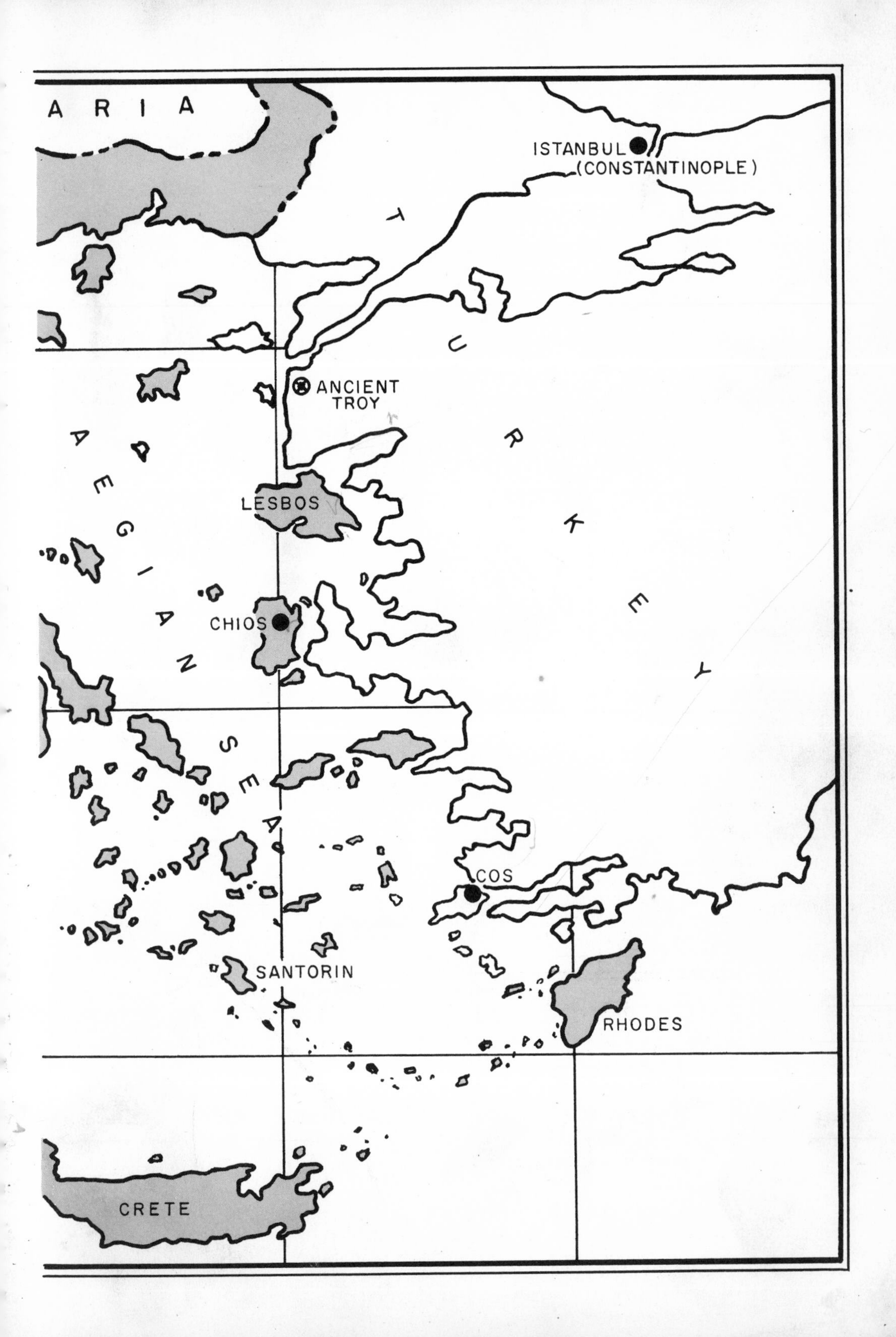
ARIA
ISTANBUL
(CONSTANTINOPLE)
TURKEY
ANCIENT TROY
AEGIAN SEA
LESBOS
CHIOS
COS
SANTORIN
RHODES
CRETE

Melos comes fine white clay from which dishes are made in a factory in Athens.

The biggest island of Greece is Crete, 173 miles long. Almost half a million people live there. The ancient Greeks believed that the powerful god Zeus was born in a cave on Mount Ida, on Crete. The first civilization in Europe began on this island. It is at a crossroads of the world, equally distant from Asia, Africa, and Europe. There were great cities in Asia and Egypt (which is in northern Africa) when the people who lived in Europe were still savages. Crete became the first great sea power in the world.

You may have heard the legend of Theseus of Athens, who went to Crete and killed a monster called the Minotaur in a winding passage in the Palace of Knossus. Theseus was rescued by the king's daughter, Ariadne, who gave him a ball of string to unwind when he entered the palace, so he could follow it back and so find his way out of the maze.

About thirty-six hundred years ago, there really was a great palace, with many passageways, at Knossus. It was destroyed by a terrible earthquake. In 1894, a British archaeologist, Sir Arthur Evans, began to dig in the ruins there. He rebuilt part of the palace, and now visitors can see what it looked like.

Between Crete and Asia Minor lie the Dodecanese, or Twelve Islands. Rhodes—for which our state of Rhode Island is named—is the

The modern village of Sparta, a few miles from the site of ancient Sparta. The forbidding mountains are the Taietos range.

These seven columns were part of a temple to Apollo in ancient Corinth.

largest of the Dodecanese. Here, in 280 B.C., was erected the Colossus of Rhodes, a huge bronze statue of the sun god Helios, 120 feet high. It was knocked down by an earthquake only fifty-three years after it was finished.

Immense pieces of the Colossus lay scattered about for more than eight hundred years. Then the Arabs captured Rhodes and sold the bronze for scrap metal. Now, nobody knows just what the Colossus looked like.

In Lindos, a pretty village on Rhodes, the narrow, winding streets are paved with black and white cobblestones, about the size of eggs, arranged in patterns. At United Nations headquarters in New York, you can see a pool that is paved with the same kind of stones, sent from Greece.

Rhodes is famous for the beautiful dishes made there, for gold and silver jewelry, and for rugs woven from goats' hair. It has wonderful bathing beaches and glorious flowers. Rhodes used to be infested with snakes. It still has many lizards, one kind so big that it is called the Dragon of Rhodes.

A few miles from the walled city of Rhodes, there is a fairyland kind of place called the Valley of Butterflies. It is a narrow ravine, down which rushes a stream. On each side are great, gnarled trees, some of which ooze a sap that smells like perfume. You see only a few butterflies (they are really moths) until you whistle or clap—then they swarm into the air by the millions, flickering orange-brown

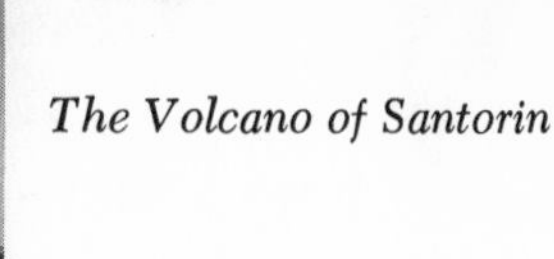

The Volcano of Santorin

in the sunlight. When they settle down, their folded wings are black with pale yellow stripes, matching the light and shadow of the forest so well that you can hardly find them.

I have mentioned earthquakes in connection with both Crete and Rhodes. Earthquakes are frequent among the Greek islands and on the mainland. The ancient people did not guess that volcanoes have a connection with earth tremors. They believed that Poseidon, god of the sea, was responsible for earthquakes, and they called him Earth-Shaker.

Modern scientists say that earth tremors in the Aegean area begin at Santorin, an island volcano that still sends up plumes of steam.

The word volcano comes from Vulcan, the name the Romans gave to the hard-working smith god whom the Greeks called Haephestus. Volcanoes, the ancient Greeks believed, were the smoking chimneys of his underground workshop.

At Santorin, ships sail into a huge round harbor that is actually the ruined crater of the old volcano. Pumice, a kind of rock thrown up by the volcano, is so light in weight that it floats on the sea like foam.

A village named Thera perches on a cliff almost a thousand feet above the sea. The only way you can get to Thera from the harbor is by means of a stone stairway. Everything has to be carried up this on the backs of donkeys.

The Island of Santorin has suffered many earthquakes. A severe one in July, 1956, tumbled houses into the sea, blocked the stairs, and left forty people dead and thousands homeless. Then a tidal wave swamped the fishing fleet and the docks.

Severe earthquakes did tremendous damage in other parts of Greece in 1953-1955. In the islands west of the mainland, 450 people were killed. The United States government made a special grant of nineteen million dollars to help the survivors rebuild.

An earthquake under the sea, in February, 1963, created a tidal wave thirty feet high that rolled into the Gulf of Corinth and wrecked scores of houses in eight villages along the shore.

Southern Greece, a peninsula shaped like a ragged leaf, is called the Peloponnesus. It is connected to the rest of the mainland by a stem called an isthmus. A canal not quite four miles long and seventy-eight feet wide, cutting across that stem, permits ships to pass from the Gulf of Corinth to the Bay of Salamis, instead of sailing two hundred miles around the peninsula.

Getting that short canal dug was a harder job than you might think. The rock there is soft, and earth slides still occur. The project was considered for 2,500 years before it was completed! A ruler of Corinth, named Periander, first thought of it in the seventh century before Christ. Six hundred years later, Julius Caesar sent engineers

The Meteora in Thessaly are monasteries — twenty-three of them — built on rock pillars. The priests and monks of the Greek Orthodox Church living in some of them have to be pulled up in a net.

Before the Corinthian Canal was dug, ships had to sail two hundred miles around the Peloponnesus or else be pushed four miles overland on greased wooden rails.

from Rome to plan a canal so his ships could take a short cut for an invasion of Persia, but he was murdered in 44 B.C., before anything could be accomplished.

Eighty-five years later, a Roman emperor named Caligula sent more engineers to look into the building of a waterway. In A.D. 41, he too was murdered—before the actual work could begin. Canal or no canal, this was fortunate, because Caligula was a dreadfully cruel man and a very bad ruler.

Twenty-seven years after that, another bad Roman emperor, Nero, really started work on the canal. He put on a spectacular ground-breaking ceremony, dug three shovelfuls of earth with a golden spade, and then turned the heavy work over to six thousand Jewish slaves, who had been brought from Judea for that purpose.

A few months later, Nero was assassinated, the work stopped, and nobody else tried to build a canal until 1882, when a French company undertook to cut through the isthmus—but gave up. Eleven years later, the Greeks themselves succeeded. Most modern ships are too big to pass through the Corinthian Canal—after all that work! But for the Greeks' own ships, most of which are small, it is a useful and important short cut.

2

The History of Greece

Democracy, which we prize so much, began in ancient Athens. Democracy means "rule by the people."

In Asia and Africa, twenty-six centuries ago, kings had complete power over their subjects. But the people of Greece were not subjects. They were citizens. They governed themselves. This was a startling new idea in the world.

All the Greeks spoke the same language and worshiped the same gods, but each of their cities was a tiny, separate nation with its own laws. Greece had no federal government, as it has now. A man from Thebes became a foreigner if he went to Athens, only fifty-five miles away.

Many of the Greek cities had kings, but they were leaders rather than rulers. For a long time, Athens was governed by a small group of wealthy noblemen. Other citizens wanted a voice in public affairs, so a wealthy merchant named Solon was selected to revise the laws in order to give more rights to more citizens. He completed his revision in 594 B.C., putting the controlling power of the city's government into the hands of a very large number of people and thus laying the foundation of democracy. (Our newspapers often speak of Congressmen as "Solons," even when they may not be as wise as the original Solon of Athens.)

About ninety years after Solon revised the laws of Athens, a nobleman named Cleisthenes reformed the constitution again, giving all citizens, rich or poor, a chance to take part in the government. The supreme authority was an assembly of five hundred men. Its members were not elected; they were chosen by lot. In this way, every citizen had a chance to become a member.

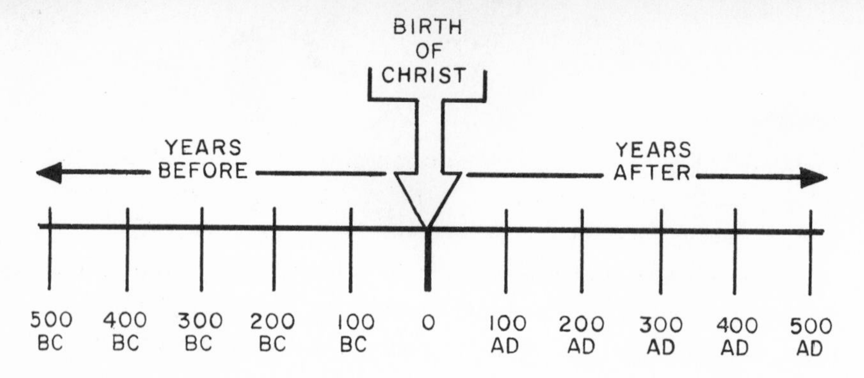

Athens achieved a more completely democratic government than even the United States has, for citizens here do not vote directly on most public issues, and most never run for office. Representatives are elected to manage government affairs. Absolute democracy, the Athenian system, could work only in a small area, where nobody had to travel very far to meetings, and where citizens had plenty of time to spend on public affairs.

Well-to-do Athenians did have time, because they did not have to work for a living. They gladly served on juries or collected taxes or performed other civic duties without pay.

Poor men were eager to serve Athens, too. A great statesman, Pericles, made it possible for them to do so. About 456 B.C., he arranged for citizens to be paid a small sum from the public treasury when they worked for Athens.

While Athens had complete democracy, the city of Sparta, in the Peloponnesus, had a form of government so severe that nobody had any freedom or enjoyment. This, too, was by consent of the citizens! The Spartans had conquered the people who lived in the province of Laconia and had made them slaves. These captives, who did all the work, were called helots. Of course they wanted freedom, and sometimes they rebelled. The Spartans were afraid of them but refused to give them any rights, just the same. To keep the helots under control, the Spartans gave up all their own personal freedom and formed a military state.

Every Spartan man was a professional soldier. He served the state from the time he was seven until he was sixty. The Spartans gloried in their ability to endure hardship and to show no emotion. Sickly babies were put out in the woods to die, because they could not be soldiers if they grew up. A woman might tell her son before a battle, "Come back with your shield or on it." Imagine having your own mother say she would rather see you dead than defeated!

Of course, the Spartans were great soldiers. They were educated for nothing but war. They had no time or desire to paint pictures, make beautiful statues, or write poetry, as other Greeks did.

In spite of such differences in government, all Greeks felt a kinship. Their name for Greece was Hellas, as it still is, and they called themselves Hellenes. Anyone who was not a Hellene was called a barbarian.

The cities of old Greece sometimes combined in leagues to fight invaders, but such alliances never lasted very long. The cities were jealous of one another.

Early in the fifth century B.C., Darius, the great king of Persia, sent heralds to all the Greek cities, demanding their surrender. Some of them gave up without a struggle, but Athens did not. The Persians invaded, and Sparta promised to send an army to aid their countrymen, but the Spartan troops arrived too late to help. On the Plain of Marathon, in 490 B.C., Athenians, all alone, won a great victory over the Persians.

Nine years later, another Persian king, Xerxes, made ready to conquer Greece. This time, most of the cities decided to work together to defend Hellas. This was a time of fear, for Xerxes had the largest military force the world had ever seen.

Several of the Greek cities sent messengers to Delphi, to ask Apollo, through his Oracle, what they should do. The Oracle's replies were ominous. She told the Spartans that they could not possibly resist the Persians and that either Sparta or a Spartan king must die. She told the Athenians that there was no hope for them at all, but when the anxious messengers asked a second time, she said they could find safety in "wooden walls." This left them puzzled. What did the Oracle mean?

The Persian hordes came into Hellas in 480 B.C., marching around the Aegean coast, with a vast fleet of ships accompanying them by sea. Leonidas, king of Sparta, with three hundred of his men, stood firm against the invaders at the narrow pass of Thermopylae, even after other Greek troops had fled or had been wiped out.

A traitor showed the Persians a path over the cliffs, and Leonidas and his three hundred Spartans were killed to the last man, as they had known they would be. A Greek inscription on a monument erected in their honor has been translated into English this way:

"Go tell the Spartans, thou that passeth by,
That here, obedient to their laws, we lie."

The battle of Thermopylae did not keep the Persians out, but the example set by the Spartans encouraged the Athenians not to give up. Xerxes' troops marched on toward Athens. Themistocles, an Athenian general, convinced his people that their ships were the wooden walls that the Oracle had said would save them. Women, children, and men too old to fight were moved to a city farther south. The men of Athens boarded their ships, except for a few who stayed on the Acropolis. The Persians killed all those who had stayed behind, destroyed the temples on the great rock, and burned all the houses.

The "wooden walls," the fighting ships of Athens, won a great victory over the Persian fleet in the Bay of Salamis. Then troops from other cities helped the Athenians to defeat the Persians in a land battle at Plataea.

Marathon, Thermopylae, Salamis, Plataea—these were shining names to the Hellenes, and they are heroic names in history now.

But the cities of Hellas went on fighting among themselves. Sparta and her allies defeated Athens in 404 B.C., ending the Peloponnesian War, which lasted for twenty-seven terrible years.

King Philip of Macedonia, a country to the north, undertook to conquer Hellas. He succeeded in 338 B.C. The Greeks, who loved liberty, were not free to govern themselves again until more than twenty-one hundred years had passed.

Philip's son, whom we call Alexander the Great, was only twenty years old when he set out to conquer the known world. He was a ruthless general. When Thebes rebelled, he destroyed the city and

The Crusaders built these huge walls around the city of Rhodes to keep their enemies out.

sold thirty thousand people into slavery.

Alexander won northern Africa and a large part of Asia. A great admirer of Greek thought, art, literature, and customs, he spread the civilization of the Hellenes wherever his armies went. Alexander had no moral right to invade the kingdoms that he conquered, but he had great talent for establishing sound governments. He died of a fever in 323 B.C., when he was only thirty-three years old, and there was no strong leader to follow him in governing his great empire. Three of his generals divided the empire among themselves, and soon the Greek cities were fighting one another again.

Alexander founded Alexandria, in Egypt, but did not live to see it built. The city became wealthy and magnificent, a center of learning for men of many nationalities. The greatest library in the world was at Alexandria, where there was also a Museum, an association of learned men, headed by a priest of the Muses. Scientists flocked to this university to learn and teach and write books.

A growing empire with its capital in Rome had gradually spread its power through much of western Europe. About 212 B.C., Rome began to take an interest in Greece. By 146 B.C., all Hellas had become an unwilling part of the Roman Empire. The Greeks remained under Roman rule for 622 years.

The Romans had a strong central government. The Roman legions brought sound laws, provided military protection, and built good roads. A Roman citizen could be sure of his rights anywhere in the vast empire.

But the Greeks hated government that was imposed upon them. Greek cities rebelled time after time. They were always defeated. When Corinth rebelled in 146 B.C., a Roman army destroyed it utterly. Later the Romans rebuilt it as a military post. In 86 B.C., Athens rebelled, and the Roman dictator, Sulla, ordered a general massacre. All Hellas become a battleground, with the people suffering and starving.

Rome's powerful empire slowly collapsed as its border outposts were overwhelmed by invading tribes of barbarians from northern Europe. In the third century after Christ, the Goths captured Athens and destroyed towns and farms as far south as Sparta. A century later, the barbarians had done so much damage that only Athens and Corinth had enough people left in them to be classified as towns. In 476, the whole western Roman Empire finally fell to the Goths from the north.

The eastern part of the empire continued, however, with its capital (built in 330 by Constantine the Great) at Constantinople, an old city that had been named Byzantium. Hellas, which was called "Old Greece," was a tiny part of this vast area, but the whole Byzantine empire was Greek in traditions and customs, and the Greek language was spoken everywhere in it.

For many centuries, Greek Constantinople was the richest, busiest, most civilized city in the world. But this didn't help the people in Old Greece. About the year 700, tribes of Slavs from Russia invaded Hellas and did much damage. Later, the Crusaders conquered the Greeks.

We think of the Crusaders as heroic knights who tried to reclaim Jerusalem, the Holy City, from the Mohammedan Arabs who had captured it in the year 637, and many of them were just that. Actually, however, quite a few of the knights were ambitious adventurers who used the Crusades as an excuse to get rich. During the Second Crusade, in 1147-1149, Norman knights captured the island of Corfu and the cities of Athens, Corinth, and Thebes.

Venice, in Italy, had become a prosperous republic whose people

This Greek boy is familiar with the transportation of the past and of the present.

were great traders. Venetians who had settled in Constantinople did a dreadful thing in 1204. They helped the knights of the Fourth Crusade sack that city, plunder the houses, and strip the great Christian churches of their treasures. Knights from France took many Greek islands for their own, set up their own governments on the mainland, and treated the people very badly.

In 1261, troops from Genoa, in Italy, helped the Greeks reclaim Constantinople, but the city never regained its old strength.

Bitterness resulting from religious differences was responsible for most of this warfare. The early Christian Church had divided into two parts in 1054, and each thought the other was wrong. The Pope, in Rome, headed the Catholic Church, and the Patriarch, in Constantinople, was head of the Orthodox Church. The Patriarch refused to acknowledge the leadership of the Pope. The two churches remain separate to this day.

Constantinople held firm against attacks by many armies, but the Byzantine Empire was doomed to fall to an invading tribe of nomadic Turks called Ottomans, or Osmanli, after one of their early chiefs, Osman. They swept into Old Greece and took Athens in 1397. Constantinople fell in 1453.

The Ottomans were determined to spread the Moslem religion, which holds that Allah is God and Mohammed is his prophet. Whenever they conquered a Christian country, they gave the people a bitter choice: to become converts to the Moslem faith or to keep

Evzones — members of the Royal Guard — in dress uniform on duty at the Tomb of the Unknown Soldier in Athens.

their own religion but have no legal rights at all. The courageous Greeks clung to their Christian faith.

The Ottomans sold enormous numbers of war captives into slavery and levied a terrible annual tribute on the Greeks—a tribute of children. Every year, a thousand Christian boys, between six and fifteen years old, had to be handed over to the Ottomans, to be brought up in the Moslem faith and trained as professional soldiers. These soldiers, called Janissaries, could not marry or have homes of their own, and, of course, they never saw their heartbroken parents again.

The Ottoman government was an absolute monarchy. The ruler, called a sultan, had complete power over everyone in his empire. None of his subjects, whether Turks or Greeks, could vote. The sultans could order anyone executed without a trial. Some of them had their own brothers murdered!

The Greeks' war of liberation from the Ottoman Empire began early in 1821. The Greeks were not united when their revolution began. They had no army, no government, no leader. Angry peasants and groups of fighting men from the mountains simply started killing their Turkish masters.

The revolution soon found a leader, Archbishop Germanos of Patras. On March 25, 1821, he blessed the flag of the Greek revolutionaries at the Monastery of Aghia Lavra. March twenty-fifth is celebrated now as Independence Day by Greeks all over the world.

Patras was the first town to revolt against the Turks. They set it afire on April 4, 1821.

The war of liberation, resulting from almost four hundred years of oppression, lasted for more than six years. On the island of Chios alone, thirty thousand Greeks were massacred. Fifty thousand women and children were taken away from Hellas by the sultan's troops, to be sold as slaves in Asia. But the people of Greece won their liberty at last.

The Ottoman Empire included large areas in southeastern Europe, and the great European powers—England, France, and Russia—felt that their interests were endangered by the Turks. Therefore, these powers wanted the Greeks to win. The last great conflict of the war was the naval battle of Navarino, in October, 1827. The united fleets of England, France, and Russia destroyed a combined fleet of Turkish and Egyptian ships.

The great powers of Europe agreed, on February 3, 1832, to recognize the independence of Greece. The new nation had no royal family, so Prince Otto of Bavaria was chosen as King of the Hellenes. He ruled for many years. His successor was a prince of Denmark.

Liberated Hellas included only a small part of the area where the Hellenes had lived for many centuries, so the Greek nation fought several wars against the sultan's empire to win the islands and mainland areas where the inhabitants were Greek. Rhodes and some of the other islands did not become part of the Greek nation until 1947.

The sultans' Moslem subjects remained under despotic rule much longer than the Greeks did. The people of Turkey did not depose their last sultan until 1922. The following year, the Republic of Turkey elected its first president.

During the Second World War, Hellas suffered severely. One-tenth of her people died. Both Italian and German armies invaded. The Italians left very soon, but the German troops stayed a long time, inflicting great damage. When they retreated from Greece in 1944, more than two thousand villages had been burned, and one-fourth of all the buildings in Hellas had been destroyed or damaged. Three-fourths of all the ships—so important to a seafaring people—had been sunk. Railroads had been ruined and large bridges dynamited. The Corinthian Canal was blocked and remained useless until it was cleared in 1949. Hundreds of olive groves and vineyards were destroyed, and livestock and even seed grain were gone. Many people starved.

Groups of tough resistance fighters, hiding in the mountains, fought the enemy in every way they could. Unfortunately, some of these guerilla fighters wanted Greece to adopt the Communist form of government, as the countries to the north had done, so, even after the great war ended in 1945, peace did not come to Hellas. There was civil war. The destruction resulting from this left 850,000 people homeless in northern Greece.

Aid from America helped to defeat the Communists. In March, 1947, President Harry Truman declared that the United States must support free people in resisting armed minorities and outside pressures. This policy, known as the Truman Doctrine, extended also to Turkey. Both Greece and Turkey received large sums of money from the United States to strengthen their governments against the Communists. The Greek army was able to defeat this enemy from within in 1949.

One of the dreadful events of the civil war was the abduction of thousands of children from Greece by the Communist-led rebels. Early in 1948, the latter announced that children between three and fourteen years old would be taken to other countries. The excuse was that they would be safer outside their native land.

The Greek government and even the United Nations were unable to prevent this mass kidnapping. By the end of 1948, the International Red Cross in Geneva estimated that nearly 23,700 Greek children had been taken from their homes and sent to Communist dominated countries.

In spite of protests at the United Nations, only a few hundred of these children were ever allowed to come home. Most of the others were never heard from again.

3

How the People Live

Both Dry and Wet Greece are so mountainous and rocky that less than a quarter of the land can be used for raising crops. This is a serious problem, because most of the people depend on farming for a living.

Commercial fishing is an important industry. Thousands of fishermen go out to sea in small boats. Often, they fish at night. The Greeks eat a great deal of fresh fish, and more than one hundred packing plants preserve many tons of the catches.

Hundreds of men earn a living by diving for sponges near the islands, but the introduction of synthetic sponges has damaged the world market for their product.

The only great city of ancient Hellas that is still important is Athens. Salonika is a big seaport up north. Patras, at the entrance to the Gulf of Corinth, is the nation's important western port for commerce with Italy. Wine and currants made from grapes raised in the Corinth area are shipped from Patras.

Greek cities, like those in America or England or Scandinavia, have big buildings and apartment houses. A businessman carrying a brief case in Athens wears the same kind of clothes as a businessman in Milwaukee, and a girl hurrying to her office job in Salonika or Patras dresses like a girl with a job in Jersey City or Rome. But most Greeks live in small villages, and the difference between village life and city life is very great.

Peasant women in Greece usually wear long, black dresses, with dark scarves covering their hair. They are seldom seen outdoors, except in the fields, working with their husbands, because they keep very busy at home. They spin and weave cloth and make their fam-

This statue, on the Acropolis, is called the Peplos Maiden. This kind of dress, called a peplos, was woven from heavy wool. Under it was a long garment of fine linen, called a chiton. The statue, made about 530 B.C., still has traces of the colors with which it was painted.

ilies' clothing, in addition to looking after their children.

Greek peasants eat meat only a few times a year. Their staple foods are olives, cheese, fruit, and bread, with fish, of course, if they live near the sea. Honey is their sweetening, and olive oil is used for cooking almost anything.

Most houses are made of stone, brick, or cement, because lumber is scarce and expensive, and they are built to keep out the summer heat. They are usually white, with a red tile roof—very pretty.

Greek boys don't have to mow lawns, because there are no lawns. Many houses have walls built clear out to the street, enclosing shady courtyards where flowers grow riotously, but there is no grass.

The Greeks love to argue. You may be sure that in ancient Greece, no important change in government was made without plenty of argument. Greek men still argue about politics and government, just as their ancestors did. Men spend their spare time in small cafes, talking endlessly about politics, making a tiny cup of thick, sweet coffee or a glass of wine last for a long time. There's an old saying, "When three Greeks get together, there are two Prime Ministers and one leader of the Opposition."

Greece doesn't have two major political parties, as the United States does. There are many parties, ranging from "left wing," or radical, to extremely conservative. Parliament—the equivalent of the Congress of the United States—includes men elected from all parties. After an election, the king appoints a prime minister whose policies are agreeable to a majority of Parliament members.

One of the things the Greeks argue about is their own language. There are two modern Greek languages, the *demotic,* or "people's" language, and *katharevousa,* or "purified." For conversation, "people's" Greek is used; it contains many Turkish, Italian, and other foreign words. Purified Greek is used officially by the government and by church dignitaries. A man named Adamantino Korais introduced the purified language at about the time of the Greek revolution. He wanted to remove foreign words, especially Turkish, from the language, in order to make the Hellenes proud of their ancient culture.

In any village, the community leaders are the president (who is chosen by elected members of the village council), the priest, and the schoolmaster. The president represents the village in its dealings with the outside world. The priest may earn his living as a farmer. On the street, priests wear long black robes and peculiar tall black caps. During the centuries of the Turkish occupation, and again during the German occupation in the Second World War, it was the priests who kept alive the proud traditions of Hellas.

Most farms are very small, because if a farmer has several sons, each of them inherits a share of the land. Very little farm machinery is used. On steep, rocky hillsides, farmers and their wives patiently

This is a flour mill on Mykonos. Hundreds of other windmills also pump water on the Aegean islands.

"This is the way we wash our clothes" in a village on Mount Pelion. Higher up the mountain, there is a cavern where, legends say, the Centaur, Chiron, educated the boy Achilles.

build up small, level patches of ground for gardens. They pile rocks in low dikes so that rainwater won't wash away the soil.

When the war was over, the United States sent agricultural experts to Greece, to show the farmers how to raise better crops and earn more money. Important improvements have resulted. For example, the Greek people consume a great deal of rice and they used to import much of it. A soil reclamation expert found great areas where rice would grow if water could be brought to the level land. He showed farmers how to make a system of irrigation ditches. As a result, five years later, Greece was growing enough rice for its inhabitants' own use—and selling five million dollars' worth to other countries besides. Raising rice requires much hand labor, so this important crop also provides work for many people who need jobs.

Farmers have raised wheat for many centuries, but on some land, cotton is a more profitable crop, because it can be made into cloth in Greek factories and sold abroad. The Greek government encourages farmers to change from wheat to cotton cultivation.

Another important crop is tobacco, which can be raised without [illegible]tion on land where other crops won't grow.

[illegible]d has too little water, and some has too much. This is a [illegible] the Greeks have had to cope with for a long time.

There used to be an immense swampy lake on the plain of Copais, in Boeotia, between Athens and Thebes. Mosquitoes swarmed there by the millions. The Boeotians used to be noted for their stupidity. But they weren't really slow-witted; actually, they were always sick and worn out from malaria, carried by the mosquitoes.

Seven hundred years ago, the French Crusaders who ruled Athens tried to drain the Copais swamps. They did not know that mosquitoes carried malaria, but they could see that the soil was fertile. They did not succeed in their drainage project, but in 1886 and 1887, French and English engineers put in a series of canals to lead the shallow water away to a river.

Now the land that was once the bed of a lake produces the richest crops of cereals and cotton in Greece, and there is also good pasture land for horses, cattle, and turkeys. Today, the Boeotian farmers can laugh at anyone who says they're stupid.

In recent years, Greek farmers have learned that it is wise to spend money for fertilizer or to borrow money in order to build irrigation systems. The increased crops enable them to pay back their loans and earn more money for their hard work.

In ancient Greece, girls had almost no education. Boys learned to read and write and count, and they memorized a great deal of poetry. All of them studied music, because every man was expected to be able to play the lyre and to sing. Boys and men spent much time

In isolated villages, women still bake bread in outdoor ovens.

The outdoor Theater of Herodes Atticus, in Athens (here set up for a concert), was built in A.D. 161.

wrestling or jumping or running races, because physical education was very important.

Now, all children must attend elementary school, beginning at age seven—and they go to school six days a week! After six years of elementary school, they may go on to "gymnasium," or secondary school, for another six years, but this is not required. It depends on whether the child intends to study at one of the universities eventually.

The girls and boys study about the same basic subjects that children in the United States do—and a lot more. They must learn ancient Greek and the two kinds of modern Greek, plus French and English, and they study Latin for eight years. No vocational courses are taught in the gymnasiums, but there are many special vocational schools.

Greece has nine schools of higher education with university standing and fourteen colleges where teachers are trained. All these institutions are supported by the Greek government, and tuition costs are low.

Because ninety-eight of every hundred people in Greece belong to the Eastern Orthodox Church, religion is taught all the way through the public schools, but the few pupils who belong to other churches are not required to take these courses.

Greek churches are beautifully decorated inside with mosaics—

pictures made of tiny bits of colored tile—on the walls and ceilings. There are no statues in them, as in Catholic churches. Instead of statues, there are icons—pictures of saints.

Of course, the ancient worship of the Olympian gods did not give way to Christianity all at once. The change took place over many years. The pagan religion taught that the dead wandered unhappily in a sad world of shadows, and the Hellenes welcomed the new faith, with its promise of life after death.

The Apostle Paul spent several years in various Greek cities, making converts. He preached in Corinth in 51 and 52 A.D. and on the Hill of Ares in Athens. In the Greek city of Ephesus, in Asia Minor, he wrote two Epistles to the Corinthians and was imprisoned by order of a Roman emperor.

On the Isle of Patmos, St. John the Divine is believed to have had the vision that he described in the Book of Revelation. At a monastery on Patmos, monks point out the grotto where he lived and wrote.

St. Andrew, another of the Apostles, preached in Patras. According to legend, he was crucified and buried there.

One of the great needs of Greece has been for roads. Building roads in the steep mountains there is very expensive. Until only a few years ago, many villages had no roads at all to connect them

Ruins of the Temple of Athena on the Acropolis of Lindos, on the Isle of Rhodes. At the right, far below, is the Bay of St. Paul, where, according to legend, the Apostle was shipwrecked during one of his missionary journeys.

with the towns where farmers could sell their produce at a profit and buy supplies they needed. Everything had to be carried on the backs of little donkeys, which plodded safely along narrow, sloping paths. Some people in the mountains never had wheat flour. They made bread from corn meal, because they could grow maize and grind it themselves.

Hundreds of miles of dirt roads have now been built throughout Greece, at low cost, so that trucks and buses can now travel where only donkeys used to go. Under the leadership of the Royal National Foundation, villagers volunteer their labor, and the Greek army lends heavy equipment, such as bulldozers. Prosperity is increasing in the once isolated villages, and residents can travel to other communities to see what the outside world is like.

The Royal National Foundation was set up on May 25, 1947, less than seven weeks after Crown Prince Paul succeeded his brother, George II, as king. The RNF helps the Greek people raise their social, educational, and living standards. It works with government authorities, and rural areas get most of the help, because that is where it is most needed.

The RNF started evening schools for boys and men who had never learned to read. It set up agricultural schools, where boys learn good farming practices, and technical schools, where they learn trades,

The peasants on the island of Skiros wear very full trousers.

A young Greek boy starts out to find business and adventure!

such as plumbing and printing. All this is free, including board. The boys must promise to go back to their villages when their courses are completed, to work for at least a year.

CARE has helped provide tools and implements for these boys, as well as sewing machines for the home economics schools, where girls from fifteen to eighteen learn to be model homemakers. They go back home afterwards and teach what they have learned about weaving, poultry raising, gardening, cooking, medical care, and other such skills.

For men who are leaders in their villages, the RNF has a three-weeks' course in community government at the *Ethniki Estia*, or National Home, near Athens. This is not a school but a discussion center, where the men selected live and talk over their villages' problems with specialists. They return to their homes filled with enthusiasm, taking fresh ideas about ways to help their neighbors live better. In the first ten years after the National Home was established, more than twelve thousand men attended these sessions.

Every year, several thousand boys and girls learn useful skills in rural centers, set up in their own villages by the RNF, which provides cooking utensils, sewing machines, hand looms, tools, and books, and also pays teachers. These centers operate for two or three years, until the village people can continue educating one another without outside help.

Many of these community projects, which are improving the lives of thousands of people, have been made possible by gifts of money contributed by Greeks who live in the United States and other countries.

4

The Animals of Greece

Artemis was the goddess of wild places and of all creatures that live there. She was Apollo's twin sister. Sometimes, in sculpture, she is shown accompanied by a deer. According to myth, she had two pet deer with golden antlers, and she used them as a team to draw her golden chariot—although it's hard to imagine how she managed a chariot in the forests where there were no roads!

Little girls, nine years old, used to be priestesses of Artemis. They were called "Little Bears," and they wore costumes made of bearskin. One of their duties was to perform a dance in honor of Artemis on certain occasions, at Brauron, twenty-three miles east of Athens. Some Athenian children, the legend tells us, had once killed a bear that Artemis liked especially well, and the angry goddess threatened the city with plague in punishment. The Little Bears dutifully danced in the temple of Artemis to keep the plague away.

In 1948, workmen who were digging to repair the foundations of an old church at Brauron found many charming, chubby statuettes of small girls and boys. The little statues were offerings from mothers who wanted Artemis to watch over their children.

Greece does not have very many large wild animals in the forests any more, but bears, lions, and dangerous wild pigs used to be plentiful. When the great army of Xerxes was marching through Thrace, in northern Greece, wild lions attacked and mauled some of the camels that carried supplies. The only lions you'll find in Greece now are in legends or marble statuary or pictures on jars and vases.

The hero Heracles (or Hercules) had to kill a legendary lion as one of the Twelve Labors he was sentenced to perform. His arrows bounced off its tough hide, his sword blade bent, and even his big club didn't hurt it. So he choked it to death and peeled off its hide with his fingernails. Heracles can always be identified in Greek art because he wears a lion's skin.

The lions that Greek sculptors made didn't look very much like real lions, especially their faces. After all, what artist can make a fierce beast stand still while he carves one just like it from a block of marble?

On the island of Little Delos, some white marble lionesses can still be seen. Once there were fourteen of them, but only five remain. They are lean and hungry-looking, with their mouths open. They have become thin as the centuries passed and the wind-blown sand wore the stone away. In the spring, masses of scarlet poppies bloom among the white marble ruins of Little Delos.

There is a charming story about this island. It used to be a sad little thing that floated around in the Aegean Sea, without any roots. A goddess named Leto was going to have a baby, but the goddess Hera hated her and said the baby could not be born in any place where the sun shone. Only humble Little Delos was willing to be a refuge for Leto, so the sea god, Poseidon, kept it covered with water, away from the sun, until Leto got there.

Leto's twins, Artemis and Apollo, were born there, under a palm tree, and ever since that time, Little Delos has been just as solid as any island anywhere.

This statue of Aesculapius, god of healing, with his snake is at Epidaurus.

Sheep are important for their meat and wool. Perhaps this patient man remembers the myth that even the god Apollo once herded sheep.

There is another story about Leto that explains the origin of frogs. She was traveling alone in Lydia, in Asia Minor, when she stopped at a pool to get a drink. Some rude men waded into the water, making it muddy. Leto called on Zeus to punish them, and they became frogs, croaking in the pool.

The ancient Hellenes had many stories about people who turned into animals. When you see a spider spinning her web, you might pity her, because she was once a princess named Arachne, who boasted too much about her skill in weaving and embroidery. Arachne unwisely challenged the goddess Athena to a contest. Athena was skillful in handwork, too, but she didn't even bother to compete with a mortal girl. She turned the princess into a spider, doomed to spin forever.

Another creature that we're told used to be human is the bird called the kingfisher, or halcyon. We still speak of "halcyon days" when we mean a happy time or beautiful weather. Halcyon was the daughter of Aeolus, guardian of the winds. She married Ceyx, son of the morning star, and they were so happy that they boasted of being like gods. The Olympians simply would not put up with this kind of presumptuous pride, so they punished the happy couple. Ceyx was drowned during a storm, and the grieving Halcyon leaped into the sea. Both became kingfishers.

The old legend said that every winter the hen kingfisher carried her dead mate to his burial. Then she built a nest of thorns, launched it on the sea, and hatched her eggs in it during the halcyon days—the seven days before and seven after the winter solstice—while her father kept the winds from blowing. This is a pretty story—but the kingfisher doesn't really build a nest. She lays eggs in holes along the shore.

Another myth explains how the peacock got all those eyes in his gorgeous, spreading tail. They first belonged to a monster called Argus. The goddess Hera became jealous of her husband, Zeus, because he admired a mortal girl named Io. Hera turned poor Io into a heifer and assigned Argus to guard her, because he had a hundred eyes and could always watch with a few of them.

Zeus told his son, the clever god Hermes, to get rid of Argus. Hermes lulled the monster into a deep sleep by playing music on a flute, and when all of Argus' eyes were closed, Hermes killed him.

Hera decorated the tail of her favorite bird, the peacock, with the hundred eyes of Argus, but she wasn't through with the girl who had become a heifer. She assigned a gadfly to torment the poor creature, and Io went galloping through the world, trying to get away from the gadfly's sting. The Ionian Sea, to the west of Greece, is named for her. She found refuge at last in Africa, where Zeus turned her into a girl again.

The imaginary creatures in the Greek legends are even more interesting than the real ones. Pegasus was a horse with wings. There were fifty Nereids—sea nymphs. One of them, Thetis, was the mother

Country women constantly spin wool into yarn, even when they're traveling. Women in Greece have been making yarn by this method for at least five thousand years. Donkeys have never been in a hurry.

of the great hero, Achilles.

Centaurs were half horse and half man. One of them, wise old Chiron, was the tutor of Achilles. A legend about a great battle between the Centaurs and a tribe of people called Lapiths was the subject matter for many scupltured decorations on ancient temples, including the one at Olympia.

Before history began, the Greeks had horses, native European ponies, but, at first, they used them only to pull chariots. Probably the legends about Centaurs began when someone got a glimpse of a man riding a horse, couldn't believe his eyes, and ran home in terror to tell about the fabulous composite creature.

Most of the imaginary monsters were dreadful. Echidne was half woman and half serpent. Cerberus, a dog with three heads, fiercely guarded the gate to the Underworld, keeping the spirits of the dead from coming back to life.

The sphinx had a lion's body, wings, and a woman's head. The Greeks got that idea from the Egyptians. There is an immense stone sphinx in Egypt, more than 4,500 years old. Most Greek statues of sphinxes are pleasant-looking, and this is strange, because in legends they weren't pleasant at all.

A hero named Oedipus, on his way to Thebes, met one who always asked travelers a riddle. If they couldn't give the right answer, she killed them. This was the riddle:

"What goes on four legs in infancy, two legs in youth, and three legs in old age?"

"A man," Oedipus answered. "He creeps on all fours as a baby, then he walks on two legs, and when he grows very old, he uses a cane."

The answer was right. The sphinx flew off, screaming with rage, and drowned herself in the sea.

Another imaginary creature was the Minotaur, which lived in the dark Labyrinth under the Palace of Minos, on the Island of Crete. This monster was half bull and half man. Every few years, the people of Athens had to send a tribute of seven youths and seven maidens to be sacrificed to the Minotaur. But Theseus, son of King Aegeus of Athens (for whom the Aegean Sea is named), went with them, killed the Minotaur, and rescued all his companions. You can walk through the passages of the Labyrinth when you visit Crete, but nobody believes now that the Minotaur ever lurked there. The Labyrinth was a kind of underground warehouse for storing grain and olive oil in great jars.

Medusa the Gorgon had snakes for hair and was so terrible that one look at her turned people to stone. The hero Perseus killed Medusa, using his shield as a mirror so that he could see where to swing his sword without looking at her.

Zeus used the fearsome head of Medusa as a center decoration for the Aegis, a strange ornament that he wore on his chest. The Aegis was made from the hide of a goat on whose milk Zeus fed when he was a baby. Sometimes he lent this ornament to his warrior daughter, Athena.

Snakes were associated with religious worship in ancient Greece. A sacred snake, kept on the Acropolis in Athens, was carefully tended by priests. It disappeared just when the Athenians were wondering whether they should leave their city because Xerxes' great army was coming. They decided that the departure of the snake was a signal that they should depart, too, and they did.

It's quite possible that the snake had nothing to say about his own leaving or staying. Probably Themistocles, who wanted the Athenians to leave for the sake of their own safety, arranged to have the snake removed.

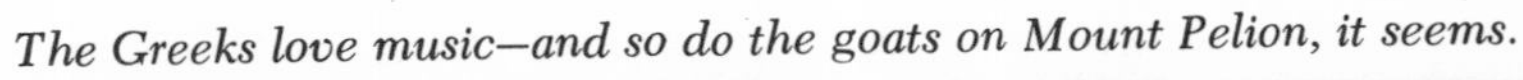

The Greeks love music—and so do the goats on Mount Pelion, it seems.

Snakes were also kept in the temples of Aesculapius, the god of healing. The sign of the physician, even now, is the caduceus, two snakes twined together. Your family doctor may have this sign on his car.

Aesculapius was a son of the god Apollo. His temples, called Aesculapions, were something like hospitals. Sick people went there, stayed for a while, and prayed for health. One of the most important of these temples was at Epidaurus, where Aesculapius was said to have been born. There was a story there that a blind man had regained his sight in the temple after two serpents licked his eyes.

Various animals were believed to be sacred to certain gods. The wise Athena had her wise little owl. Ares, the fierce war god, had the wolf, the vulture, and the woodpecker. The smiling goddess of love, Aphrodite, rode through the air in a chariot drawn by doves. Zeus had his lordly eagles, well suited to the king of the gods.

Greece still has many small wild animals and many songbirds, and the sea is very rich in living things. Purple dye—the royal color in ancient times—was made from a shellfish called murex. This dye ranged from blue to dull crimson and often wasn't what we call purple. Each murex yields only a few drops of a creamy fluid, which changes color when it is exposed to light. After that, the fluid had to be condensed by using steam. The process was so slow and expensive that only very rich people could afford to wear clothing dyed "purple."

More than 2,500 years ago, a man in Athens had this statue of himself, called the Calf Bearer, made for a gift to the temple of Athena. It was then brightly painted.

Pelicans are not native to Greece, but this one came out of the sky to the island of Mykonos and made himself at home.

You may not think the octopus is a thing of beauty, but the ancient Greeks did. This sea creature has eight long, squirmy arms, and its head and body are combined in a bump that has two big, staring eyes. Greek artists saw grace in its flexibility and often used pictures of it to decorate vases or walls.

Octopi live along the shore, in rocky places where they can protect their soft bodies in crevices and holes. Some are very tiny; others are as much as fourteen feet across their outspread arms. Fishermen kill them and then beat them against rocks for many hours, to make the flesh tender enough to eat after it is cooked.

Another sea food that is delicious (after you get used to the idea) is squid, which the Greeks call *kalamarakia*. Small ones, fried, make a tasty forkful. Bigger ones are sliced before cooking and look, on your plate, something like fried onion rings.

The squid has ten arms, or tentacles, hanging from its body all in one direction, not spread out like the arms of the octopus. There are really enormous squid, as much as seventy-five feet long, but nobody eats them. Who wants to go near a thing like that?

The playful dolphin is common in the seas off Greece. It is not a fish but an air-breathing mammal, like the whale. The dolphin is six to eight feet long and has a beak with a built-in smile. Dolphins live in herds or schools and leap through the air in graceful curves, playing through the waves. The artists of old Hellas used dolphins in mural paintings, in statuary, on coins, and in decorations on vases.

Greek seamen admire the friendly, playful dolphins and do not kill them.

5

The Plants of Greece

The saddest of the myths of Greece concerns the grief of the goddess Demeter for her lost daughter, Persephone. The story is not sad all the way through, though.

Persephone was dancing with a group of nymphs in a flowery meadow when the earth opened and a team of black horses came galloping up from the depths, drawing a chariot. The driver was fearsome Hades, god of the Underworld and keeper of the dead. He seized the screaming girl, and the earth closed over them.

Demeter searched for nine days, constantly calling for her child. On the tenth day, she learned what had happened. A boy named Triptolemus, who herded his father's cattle, knew a man who had seen the kidnapping take place.

The anxious mother vowed that the earth should remain barren until Persephone was restored to her. All mankind would starve. Hades grudgingly agreed to bring back the girl if she had not tasted any food in the Underworld. But Persephone had eaten a few seeds of a pomegranate. Therefore, for part of every year, she must return to the kingdom of the god Hades. That time is winter, when Demeter mourns again, and the fields are bleak and bare.

Demeter gave Triptolemus a handful of seed grain, a wooden plow, and a chariot drawn by serpents and instructed him to travel all over the world, teaching mankind how to sow and reap.

The ancient people believed that Demeter found Persephone at Eleusis, fourteen miles west of Athens. Now it is a small town with several busy factories, but, long ago, it was a great religious center for the worship of Demeter. We can see the reason for this: the people believed they would starve if the goddess of the fruitful earth did not look favorably on the human race.

The Mysteries of Demeter were celebrated at Eleusis by hundreds of thousands of people through many centuries. They really were mysteries, too. None of those people ever told what really happened in that strange religious ceremony!

In spite of what happened to Persephone, Greek mothers encourage their children to eat pomegranate seeds, which are covered with a juicy, acid-flavored pulp. These seeds are believed to be a tonic to purify the blood. Pomegranate fruit is round and dull red, growing on shrubs with glossy leaves. The flowers are trumpet-shaped and fiery red.

Demeter is sometimes called the goddess of the corn, but corn, in this sense, means any kind of grain. The tall plant that we call corn is properly called maize. It grows in Greece now, but it is not native there. Maize was first grown by the Indians in the Americas. Two other important crops that originated in this part of the world and are now cultivated in Greece are tomatoes and tobacco.

Wheat, barley, spelt, and millet are cereals that have been raised in Greece for food since before history began. The word "cereal" comes from Ceres, the Romans' name for Demeter.

Grapes are an important product of Greece. Some varieties are pressed to extract the juice, from which wine is made. Others are dried and become currants—small raisins. The word "currant" comes from the place name, Corinth. For many miles around Corinth, you

Demeter gives some grain to Triptolemus, with instructions to teach mankind how to plant and harvest it. At the right is Demeter's daughter, Persephone.

can see green fields of grape vines, trained on stakes and kept clipped so that they do not grow very tall. In courtyards, grape vines are allowed to grow naturally, to make pleasant shade.

Many kinds of fruit trees that grow in Greece were imported long ago from other countries. The peach used to be called "Persian apple," and the apricot was "Armenian apple." Figs, oranges, and lemons came from other countries.

The olive tree, immensely important now, as it was in ages past, is native to that area, but the ancient people believed that the goddess Athena gave it to them. To us, olives are tasty little treats served at picnics, but in Greece and many other countries they take the place of meat.

There are hundreds of types of olive trees. One of the best varieties is named for Athena herself. Most kinds produce fruit that is better for making oil than for eating. Olive oil is used by the Greeks in cooking, where people of other nations may use butter or vegetable shortening or lard.

Newly planted trees bear a few olives after four to eight years, but a full crop cannot be expected until the tree is twelve to fifteen years old. Even on an old, mature tree, the harvest is unpredictable —it may be good or bad. Nobody understands the reason for this,

These feathery trees are umbrella pines on the Isle of Skiathos. Quince, olive, and fig trees also grow on this fertile island.

This Corinthian girl is hanging clusters of grapes to dry for currants.

but agriculture specialists are trying to find out, so that growers can be sure of a steady, abundant crop.

Olive growers patiently prune and graft their trees, year after year, using the trimmed-off branches for fuel, and planting new trees when the very old ones die. The Royal National Foundation maintains several nurseries where olive saplings are grown and supplies these at cost to farmers. There are olive groves in Greece that are a thousand years old.

The olive tree has broad leaves but is evergreen. It blossoms in May. The fruit, which contains a single seed, or "stone," turns from dark green to straw color in October and is harvested then, if the fruit itself is to be eaten. If the olives are to be pressed to make oil, they are left on the trees until January or February.

Some farmers raise mulberry trees because the leaves serve two purposes. The green leaves provide food for silkworms, which are raised in sheds, and the dried leaves are fed to goats and sheep in the winter.

The stately cypress, which may grow to a height of more than one hundred feet, is named for Kyparissos, a boy who grieved so much over the death of his pet deer that he was changed into a tree.

The laurel tree, which grows abundantly in Greece, was considered sacred to Apollo. Wreaths of laurel were used in ancient Greece to crown persons who won fame as poets or artists. The word laurel (which comes from Latin) is found in some English words. For ex-

Agave, or century plant, is sometimes called "no death" because it lives so long. This bathing beach is on Cephalonia, largest island in the Ionian Sea.

ample, an honored poet is sometimes called a poet laureate, and a baccalaureate service is still part of the formal graduation ceremony when students finish high school or college. The Greeks call laurel "daphne," after a nymph by that name who turned into a tree.

There are several kinds of laurel. One is a bush that we call sweet bay. We sometimes use a dried bay leaf as seasoning in food, so laurel, which once symbolized great honor, has come down in the world!

The Oriental plane tree, which lives to a great age, is common in Greece. "May you live as long as a plane tree," the Greeks say. On the Isle of Cos there is an ancient plane tree with a twisted trunk more than fifty feet around. Its spreading branches are propped up with long stakes to keep them from breaking.

The people of Cos say that this is the very same tree under which the first doctor, Hippocrates, used to sit while he lectured to his medical students. He died more than 2,300 years ago! A forestry expert in Athens told me that this may, indeed, be the same tree that shaded Hippocrates. Plane trees really do live that long.

A kind of chewing gum that people in the Aegean area like is made from the sweet, sticky sap of mastic trees. Four million of these trees grow on the Isle of Chios. Mastic gum is also used as a basis for paint and varnish.

The flowering trees, vines, and shrubs of Greece are very beautiful, and most of them are very fragrant. They include bougainvillaea, mimosa, acacia, sycamore, jasmine, hibiscus, and oleander.

A serious problem in Greece is the poor quality of its forests. Two-thirds of the country is mountainous, good for forests and not much else, but much of this area has no trees big enough to cut into lumber. Also, where these hillsides are not protected by trees, rain washes the soil down into the streams, and it goes finally into the sea and is wasted. This leaves the steep slopes with their rocks almost bare, and nothing can grow there except useless weeds.

As a result of all this, wood for lumber and fuel is scarce and expensive throughout Greece. During the Second World War, the German troops who invaded the country ruthlessly destroyed about one-fourth of the forests. They set fire to large areas, to drive out the resistance fighters.

Almost two-thirds of the forest land of Greece is now owned by the government, and even the privately owned forest areas are managed by the Forest Service, a division of the Ministry of Agriculture. Trees may not be cut down without official permission.

Goats make this problem worse. They eat the tiny seedlings that would grow into big trees if left alone. But the Greek people badly need their goats and sheep and sometimes let them feed in the forests because there is not enough pasture land elsewhere.

In the mountains, there are many torrents—unpredictable, untamed streams that go dry in hot weather but carry a flood of fast-

The Island of Corfu, west of Greece, has its own little islands, like these. Odysseus was washed ashore on Corfu and was rescued by the king's daughter, Nausicaa. Century plant in the foreground.

flowing water after a heavy rain. These torrents result from the loss of forests, and they make that loss worse. After a rain, they sometimes wash away soil, rocks, roads, and bridges, and they may even drown people and livestock. Foresters, working under the direction of the Ministry of Agriculture, are trying to control the torrents by building small dams across the streams. These dams help to retain the fertile soil and prevent more damage, but building them is very expensive.

Millions of small trees have been planted on bare mountain sides so that new forests will grow. A hybrid poplar is used extensively in reforestation, because this tree grows fast and matures early.

The Royal National Foundation has enlisted the help of school children and Boy Scouts to plant tiny trees, under the supervision of the Ministry of Agriculture. The RNF oversees the planting of a million little trees a year.

Many kinds of cactus grow in Greece. Some of them are more useful than you might think possible. One kind, with round leaves about the size of a dinner plate, is often planted around garden patches. The thorny clumps serve as tight fences to keep out destructive animals. The fruit of this cactus makes very good salad—but look out for those sharp thorns!

Another kind, with tall, spiky leaves, is used for fences, too, and

Picture at left, taken in 1934, shows check dams built to prevent soil wash. One at right, taken twenty-five years later, shows increased growth of trees and other vegetation as a result of stopping erosion.

The White Tower in Salonika is also called the Bloody Tower, because about two hundred years ago the Sultan ordered the massacre of some of his soldiers who were imprisoned here. The slim, graceful tree is a cypress.

the fiber of the leaves can be dried and twisted into rope.

A weed that was once very useful is fennel. The stalks, which sometimes grow to a height of five feet, have a pithy center that burns slowly. Not very many years ago, country people who had no matches carried fire in fennel stalks when they went on journeys.

A myth tells us that mankind first obtained fire when Prometheus brought it to earth from heaven in a fennel stalk, although Zeus had forbidden him to do so. For this defiance, Zeus had Prometheus chained to a rock, where vultures fed on his liver until the hero Heracles (or Hercules) set him free.

Poor people used to eat the young shoots of a weed called mallow and the bulbs of asphodel, another very common weed that grows in dry places. Asphodel, with so pretty a name, should be a beautiful plant, but it is tall, stiff, and scraggly. It has pale pink flowers. The ancient Hellenes associated it with the dead and believed that there were fields of asphodel in the Underworld.

More than eight thousand kinds of wildflowers flourish in Greece. Many of the flowers that grow in our gardens are connected with myths. Iris was the bright-winged goddess of the rainbow. Narcis-

This plane tree on the Isle of Cos is said to be more than 2,400 years old.

sus was a handsome boy who fell in love with his own reflection in a pool. Heliotrope, which turns toward the sun, was once a nymph who stood adoring Apollo until she took root.

Here's a little story about plain old ordinary cabbage. Zeus's wife, the goddess Hera, was often angry with him, and she didn't hesitate to say so. The first cabbage grew where a drop of sweat fell from his forehead when Hera was scolding him!

Two horses and a mule are treading the harvested grain to separate the kernels from the straw. Sometimes threshing is done with a team of oxen pulling a heavy wooden sled over the grain.

6

Our Heritage from Greece

The Storytellers. The poet we call Homer is a man of mystery. There is a tradition that he was born on the Isle of Chios and that he was blind. He lived a very long time ago; nobody knows even in what century. The important thing is that he was one of the greatest storytellers in the world.

Homer wrote two books—long, exciting stories called *The Iliad* and *The Odyssey,* about the Greeks' legendary siege of Troy and what happened after the city fell. He told about great heroes, Achilles and Hector and Odysseus and Menelaus, whose wife was the beautiful Helen. The Olympian gods took part in the Trojan war, too.

Homer didn't really write. He sang his stories to the music of a lyre, from memory, and other men learned them and sang them. A long time later, someone wrote them down. The works of Homer used to be called "the bible of Hellas," because all educated men knew them thoroughly and quoted from them constantly.

There's another famous man about whom we know very little. When we speak of sour grapes, or killing the goose that laid the golden eggs, we are referring to fables by Aesop. He told hundreds of these little stories. Aesop was probably a foreign slave who lived in Greece in the sixth century before Christ.

The Lovers of Wisdom. Today, we learn many things in school, as a matter of course, that even the wisest men in the world did not know in ancient times. Somebody had to find these things out. The Greek philosophers, "lovers of wisdom," were pioneers of the intellect. They wondered about matters that nobody had thought about before. They were searchers for truth. They tried to find out about all kinds of things—the shape of the earth, how the stars move, the nature of the soul.

The first philosopher whose name we know was Thales. He was born in Miletus, in Asia Minor, about 640 B.C. and died in 546 B.C. He traveled widely, always asking questions. In Egypt, he learned geometry and calculated the height of the pyramids. Thales also studied astronomy and astonished his neighbors by predicting accurately that an eclipse of the sun would occur on a certain day in 585 B.C.

Socrates of Athens, who was born in 469 B.C., was a homely man with a snub nose. He was a wise and wonderful man who spent his life searching for the truth. "The unexamined life is not worth living," he once said. He believed that truth and goodness are real, not just something to talk about.

Socrates constantly discussed all kinds of things with the young men of Athens, teaching them to question and to think. He refused to accept pay for his teaching but earned a living as a sculptor. He was a good citizen. He could have escaped from prison after he was sentenced to death, but he preferred to obey the laws of his city.

This great man was charged with impiety, because he did not believe completely in the official religion of the Olympian gods, and with corrupting the young men by political teaching. Socrates was tried by a large jury of Athenian citizens and condemned to die by drinking poison made of hemlock, a plant of the carrot family. Here is part of his eloquent address to the court:

"O judges, be of good cheer about death, and know of a certainty that no evil can happen to a good man either in life or after death. He and his are not neglected by the gods, nor has my own approaching end happened by mere chance. But I see clearly that the time has arrived when it is better for me to die and be released from trouble."

Surrounded by his sorrowing friends, Socrates drank the poison and died at peace and without pain in 399 B.C.

Plato, a devoted pupil of Socrates, was twenty-eight years old when his great master died. Plato wrote down the teachings of Socrates, and all his life he thought about the principles of govern-

Hippocrates, the first doctor, seems to say, "I'll try to help you get well."

ment. One of his books is *The Republic,* a plan for an ideal state. It is not *our* idea of an ideal state, however. We demand more individual freedom than Plato would allow.

In 387 B.C., he founded the Academy, the first university in the world, in Athens. This school, which taught science and philosophy, continued for more than nine hundred years, until the Byzantine Emperor Justinian ordered all the schools in Athens closed in A.D. 529.

Plato taught that character and good will are not enough to solve human problems unless they are accompanied by clear, scientific thought. He died at eighty, in 347 B.C.

Aristotle, one of the greatest thinkers who ever lived, was born in northern Greece in 385 B.C. At eighteen, he went to Athens to study in the Academy, and he remained there for twenty years. In 343 B.C., he was invited to become the tutor of young Prince Alexander, in Macedonia; he taught Alexander for three years, until the boy was sixteen.

Aristotle then returned to Athens and founded his own school, the Lyceum. He spent his life wondering, learning, teaching, and writing. He extended the boundaries of human thought in almost every field. He wrote on logic, poetry, art, psychology, philosophy, natural science, ethics, and politics.

He outlined a "ladder of nature," starting with plants and simple animals and ending with man. He tried to find out how living things differ and how they are alike. This was an enormous undertaking, as you will see if you try to tell all the ways in which an oyster, for example, is different from yourself and all the ways in which it is like you.

Aristotle's brilliant pupil, Alexander, did not forget him. From distant lands, where Alexander led his conquering armies, he sent samples of strange plants and animals back to Athens for his old teacher to study. Aristotle died in 322 B.C., a year later than Alexander the Great.

The first botanist in the world was Theophrastus, who was born about 370 B.C. on the Isle of Lesbos. He became a pupil of Plato at the Academy and a friend of Aristotle. Theophrastus wrote books about plants—their appearance, where they grew and how, the ways in which one plant differs from another, and how they can be used. He died about 285 B.C.

The Mathematicians. Greek thinkers did not invent mathematics, but they contributed greatly to it—mostly for the fun of figuring things out, rather than for practical purposes. They must have had a dreadful time with plain arithmetic, because numbers had not been thought of yet.

Pythagoras combined mathematics with religion. There were many strange stories told about him; it was said that he could hear "the music of the spheres," the sounds made by the stars. His birth

This is a miniature reconstruction of the way Olympia probably used to look, with buildings for athletes and trainers by the temple, and many statues.

and death dates are not known with certainty. He was born between 585 and 565 B.C., and died between 495 and 470 B.C. He founded a brotherhood of young men to whom he taught what he knew and believed, but they had to swear never to tell any outsiders.

Mathematics did not remain secret, however. Over the door of Plato's Academy, about a century later, was this inscription: "Let no one ignorant of geometry enter."

We know even less about Euclid, a later Greek philosopher and mathematician, than we do about Pythagoras. About 300 B.C., Euclid taught geometry in Alexandria, Egypt, and wrote a series of textbooks, which he called the Elements. Some of his work is still taught in our schools.

You have no doubt heard about Archimedes before this. He is the man who solved a problem while in the bathtub and ran, dripping, out into the street, shouting, "Eureka!"—meaning, "I have found it!"

Archimedes was born in Syracuse, in Sicily, about 287 B.C. He liked to make practical use of mathematics. He invented a pulley and an endless screw for raising water to a higher level. The principle of Archimedes' screw is still used in the Netherlands for draining low land.

In the year 212 B.C., a Roman army conquered Syracuse, but Archimedes, sitting in the market place, studying some figures he had drawn in the sand, paid no attention until a soldier approached. "Disturb not my circle!" the old philosopher warned, but the soldier killed him.

The First Doctor. The first scientific medical doctor in the world was Hippocrates, who said it was all nonsense to blame the gods for diseases. He believed that a doctor should help the body heal itself, and he kept careful case histories of his patients and wrote many books to help future doctors understand sickness. A remark of his we often quote, even now, is: "One man's meat is another man's poison," meaning that what is good for one person may be bad for another.

Almost nothing is known about Hippocrates except the books he wrote. He was born on the Isle of Cos, about 460 B.C., and died in Thessaly about 377 B.C.

To this day, Doctors of Medicine take the noble Hippocratic Oath when they receive their degrees. Here are parts of it:

> I swear by Apollo the physician, and Aesculapius, and Health, and All-Heal, and all the gods and goddesses that, according to my ability and judgment, I will keep this oath and this stipulation:
>
> To recognize him who taught me this art equally dear to me with my parents. . . . I will give no deadly medicine to anyone if asked. . . . With purity and with holiness I will pass my life and practice. . . . Whatever, in connection with my professional practice, or not in connection with it, I may see or hear in the life of men which ought not to be spoken of abroad, I will not divulge, as reckoning that all such should be kept secret.

The First Plays. When you see a play on the stage or watch a motion picture or a television drama, keep in mind that you owe a debt to the ancient Greeks for the pleasures they have passed on to you. They invented the drama. Plays were originally part of a public religious festival, honoring the wine god, Dionysus.

The Greek theaters were out of doors, and the audience sat on stone benches built along a hillside. The stage was not a raised platform, like ours. It was a sunken circle, called the orchestra. In the orchestra, the actors (who were always men) recited magnificent poetry. A chorus also took part—but don't think of this chorus as being made up of gaily dressed dancing girls. The Greek chorus consisted of twelve or fifteen men, dressed all alike, who chanted their lines and moved in slow, dignified patterns.

The audience never saw any violent action. If some character in a play was killed (and this often happened), the deed took place off stage and a messenger ran in and told about it.

We still read, in translation, the moving tragedies written by three Athenian playwrights. Aeschylus, who was born in 525 B.C., fought in the Battle of Marathon and asked to have this fact recorded on his tombstone, because it seemed more important to him than the great plays he wrote. He died in 455 B.C.

At ancient Olympia, a modern Greek athlete receives a torch that he will carry to the site of the Games, wherever they are being held in the world.

Sophocles was born about 497 B.C. and died in 405 B.C., the year before Sparta defeated Athens in the Peloponnesian War. He was a very pious man. When a snake came into his house, he was pleased and proud, because he believed that his vistor was the god Aesculapius.

Euripides was born in 480 B.C., at Salamis, on the very day of the great sea battle there, and died at seventy-four, in Thrace, far from home. He has been called "the poet of the world's grief."

Aristophanes, who was born about 446 B.C., wrote comedies, in which he often made fun of famous people, like the wise Socrates. He wrote some of his plays during the Peloponnesian War, when the Athenians really needed something to make them laugh and forget their troubles for a while. He died in 380 B.C.

The First Historians. One subject we all study in school now is history. The most learned men in the ancient western world could not do this until Herodotus wrote his books, about the middle of the fifth century before Christ. There was no history that anybody could refer to before that. There were old stories, of course, but they were at least partly imaginary. If anyone wanted to know what had really happened in the past, he couldn't find out. Nobody had ever written down the facts.

Herodotus, who was born at Helicarnassus, in Asia Minor, decided to tell about the wars the Greeks waged with the Persians. Few men who knew about them from experience were still alive, but Herodotus did the best he could—and it was something that no one else in Europe had ever tried to do. We don't know just when he was born—perhaps about 485 B.C. He died about 430 B.C.

The second historian was Thucydides. He undertook to write about the Peloponnesian War, between Athens and Sparta, while it was still going on, so we might call him the first war correspondent. He was probably in his late twenties when he began this work, in 431 B.C.

Thucydides was elected to serve as a general of the army of Athens in 424 B.C., but he failed to reach a certain place with his ships in time to save it from the enemy. Although this was not his fault, he was banished from Athens as punishment. He continued to write his history, and he was still living when the war ended, but he did not tell the end of it. Maybe he felt too bad, because Athens was defeated. He died about 400 B.C.

The Parthenon was begun in 447 B.C., and finished in 438, except for the sculptured decorations, which took another six years. This great temple was built on the site of an older Parthenon that the Persians had destroyed.

The architects, Ictinus and Callicrates, understood optical illusion. Many of the seemingly straight lines of this structure are really subtle curves; the outer columns, which look vertical, lean slightly inward. This fool-the-eye effect was a triumph of architecture. If these lines were really straight, the building would not look right.

Great Sculptors. Most of the names of the ancient sculptors have been lost, but the most famous one was Phidias, who was born in Athens in 498 B.C. and died when he was sixty-six. His works included two immense statues of Athena. One, of bronze, stood in the open on the Acropolis. Sailors far out at sea could see the sun glint on the spear of the city's patron goddess. The other, inside the Parthenon, was more than forty feet high. It was made of wood overlaid with ivory and gold.

Phidias was the general overseer for the construction of the Parthenon, and he made some of its wonderful decorations. Beautiful fragments of them, known as the Elgin Marbles, can be seen now in the British Museum in London. Among the choicest of these are the spirited, rearing horses with their fine riders.

The reason they're there is that Lord Elgin, who was England's ambassador to Turkey, removed them from the Acropolis in 1801 with permission from the Turkish government. This was when the Ottomans were still in control of Greece. The Greeks—and many other people—would like to have the Elgin Marbles returned to Athens now. If Lord Elgin had not taken them away, however, they would surely have been destroyed during the Greek revolution.

Another famous sculptor was Praxiteles, who lived about a century later than Phidias. His white marble statue of the god Hermes holding the infant Dionysus is at Olympia. It stands now in a big box of sand so that it won't shatter if an earthquake should topple it.

Sculpture of the time of Phidias—the Golden Age—is noted for its dignity and serene grace. As artists perfected their skill, their work became more lifelike—which doesn't necessarily mean better. A famous group in the Vatican Museum in Rome shows the Trojan priest Laocöon and his two sons being crushed by huge serpents. This Greek work, dating from about 150 B.C., is certainly realistic, showing extreme physical exertion, but critics admire it less than the restrained, stylized figures of earlier centuries.

The pleasant curve of the mouth in very old statues, such as the Calf Bearer (shown elsewhere in this book), is called "the archaic smile." This sweet, mysterious smile appears even in distinctly unamusing situations—for example, on the face of a wounded warrior who is obviously dying.

The Erechtheum, the beautiful little temple at the left on the Acropolis at Athens was sacred to both Athena and Poseidon. The Parthenon is at the right.

The Olympic Games. The original Olympic Games were held every four years, starting about 776 B.C., in honor of Zeus at his great temple at Olympia. Winners in these athletic contests received no prize except an olive wreath, but they were idolized by the people of the cities from which they came. When a winner went back home, his fellow citizens didn't take him in through the city gate. They tore down part of the wall and carried him triumphantly through the gap, signifying that with so great a man among them, they needed no other protection from their enemies.

The month in which athletes and spectators traveled to and from Olympia was held sacred. All wars between Greek cities stopped during that time. The games were celebrated for the last time in A.D. 393, so they had gone on for 1,169 years!

Then in 1896, Baron Pierre de Coubertin, a French nobleman, revived the Games as a way of building friendship among all the countries of the world. The Olympics are no longer Greek; they are international. They have been held in many different nations, every four years since 1896, except when the two World Wars were in progress. Baron de Coubertin died in 1937. His heart is buried at Olympia, under a monument erected in his honor, near the tumbled ruins of the temple of Zeus.

The entire western world of the present has been deeply influenced by the Greeks—by their profound thinking, their creative genius, and their heroism. May the future of Greece be as golden as her past!

This modern monument at Thermopylae honors Leonidas and the three hundred Spartans who died there in 480 B.C., defending the pass. Three hundred Greek-Americans gave this memorial to their native land.

Index

Dorothy M. Johnson

was born in McGregor, Iowa, and grew up in Whitefish, Montana, in the Rocky Mountains. She is not quite comfortable unless there are some mountains around —which is one reason why she likes Greece. "Parts of that country resemble our own Rockies," she says, "but we don't have any ancient marble temples."

After graduation from Montana State University, Dorothy Johnson worked as a magazine editor in New York. Then she returned joyfully to Montana, where, she says, "We have all this wonderful space with practically nobody in it. All of Montana has fewer people than the city of Seattle."

Miss Johnson is now an assistant professor of journalism at her alma mater and secretary-manager of Montana State Press Association. She has written—chiefly about the West—for many magazines. All of her books, with the exception of *Greece: Wonderland of the Past and Present*, are concerned with the West, including *Famous Lawmen of the Old West*. Two motion pictures—*The Hanging Tree* and *The Man Who Shot Liberty Valance*—and several television programs have been based on stories she wrote.